Friends to the End

Other Books by Bradley Trevor Greive

The Blue Day Book

The Blue Day Journal and Directory

Dear Mom

Looking for Mr. Right

The Incredible Truth About Mothers

The Meaning of Life

Priceless: The Vanishing Beauty of a Fragile Planet

Tomorrow

The Book for People Who Do Too Much

The Blue Day Book for Kids

Dear Dad

A Teaspoon of Courage

The Simple Truth About Love

Friends to the End for Kids

Dieting Causes Brain Damage

Every Day Is Christmas

A Teaspoon of Courage for Kids

Thank You for Being You

I'm Sorry . . . My Bad!

Why Dogs Are Better Than Cats

Friends to the End

THE TRUE VALUE OF FRIENDSHIP

BRADLEY TREVOR GREIVE

**Andrews McMeel
Publishing, LLC**

Kansas City • Sydney • London

Andrews McMeel Publishing, LLC
an Andrews McMeel Universal company
1130 Walnut Street, Kansas City, Missouri 64106

www.andrewsmcmeel.com

Book design by Holly Ogden

11 12 13 14 15 WKT 10 9 8 7 6 5 4 3 2 1

ISBN: 978-1-4494-1406-1

Library of Congress Control Number: 2010937881

Attention: Schools and Businesses
Andrews McMeel books are available at quantity discounts with bulk purchase for educational, business, or sales promotional use. For information, please e-mail the Andrews McMeel Publishing Special Sales Department: specialsales@amuniversal.com

Bradley Trevor Greive loves animals and proudly supports the Taronga Foundation. To find out how you too can easily make a difference by becoming a zoo parent or making a donation toward vitally important research and breeding programs, visit the Taronga Foundation Web site: www.tarongafoundation.org

PHOTO CREDITS

For those who believed in me
when I no longer believed in myself.
For those who swept the darkness from my face with a smile.
For those who exchanged my burdens for their heartfelt joy
and never sought a better bargain.
For those whose love and laughter gave me wings
and a blue sky.
For those I cannot thank enough
in this lifetime or the next.

For my friends.

Acknowledgments

It recently dawned on me that my parents and I have become close friends. Not that we weren't close before, but gradually over the past few years, the familial roles have relaxed to the point where only mutual love and respect remain unchanged. Now we seek each other's company for reasons that completely transcend family loyalty. Best of all, our pleasant post-dinner conversations no longer end with anyone being told to go to bed . . . so far (I'm watching Dad closely). Of course, there is still so much I can learn from them, but now, perhaps, there is a little they can learn from me as well.

However, not only am I enjoying the company of two remarkable people even more than before, the greater truth is that I have suddenly seen *all* my friends in a whole new light. I now realize how important my friends have been in every aspect of my life; in many ways my friends were my family, too. Or to put it another way, I see now that I have surrounded myself with a family of friends. I have a great deal to thank them for, and I suspect a lot of people feel the same way—which is why I have so enjoyed writing this small but special book about the true value of friendship.

Over the years I have found a home with more than one hundred renowned and supportive publishing families throughout the world. I am forever grateful to these wonderful creative collaborators who have brought my work to life and, in doing so, made my life possible. I thank them all from the bottom of my heart, and I also raise my glass for a special toast to honor Christine Schillig, in the United States, and Jane

Palfreyman, in Australia, my two most eloquent and eagle-eyed editorial guardians. Like all the books in *The Blue Day Book* series, *Friends to the End* would be nothing without its superb images. I encourage everyone to celebrate the photographers and the photo libraries that have given so much to this book by seeking out their updated contact details posted at www.btgstudios.com.

My peacetime duty commanding an airborne rifle platoon in the Australian Army was astonishingly brief and pleasantly uneventful—serving, as I did, a quiet, sun-kissed nation that shares all its political borders with dolphins. Nevertheless, I have a genuine understanding of how important friends are when the world is turned inside out around you. My army buddies and I have always been there for each other and always will be.

When I think of having friends to the end, I must acknowledge that no one has stood by my side in the publishing world like my celebrated literary agent and certified hero, Sir Albert J. Zuckerman of Writers House, New York. When I was little more than an unknown Tasmanian author who could barely lift my knees in time to music, Al grabbed my drooping shoulders, shook my modest talent like an inflatable ferret, and taught me to tap dance on the world stage. I know I could not have come nearly as far without him.

Beyond our love of literature I suppose the obvious thing that binds Al and me together is our common history of military service. Of course, it is Sir Albert who really embodies the finest qualities of the poet warrior. A few weeks after he joined thousands of stouthearted Marines storming the Normandy beaches during World

War II, Al found himself wounded and cut off from his unit after an unsuccessful but confusing Axis counterattack. Deep behind enemy lines, Al collapsed in the only freestanding dwelling he could find—an abandoned patisserie. Scrounging among the disheveled storeroom for something to eat, he discovered a blond Pekingese puppy quivering inside a tin of milk powder. "*La Petite Chenille*" (the little caterpillar) was stitched carefully onto her handmade collar.

The puppy was incredibly sensitive to noise and would forewarn Al of incoming fire by cowering under the bed well before the shrieking shells had come to the attention of his highly tuned combat senses. It wasn't long before this friendly little caterpillar had crawled into Al's heart for good, her companionship keeping his hopes and dreams intact.

After the duo was finally rescued by British troops, they spent many weeks in a field hospital where Al discovered that his fluffy friend also had a discerning ear for music, with a strong preference for Edith Piaf. The two sang Piaf's beautiful laments together with Chenille howling musically. Soon they had choreographed an entire song-and-dance routine. Al's spirit and health quickly revived while his puppy became plump and alert.

After the war Al brought Chenille back with him to America where they performed at Carnegie Hall in New York and, after typically scathing opening-night reviews, together they overwhelmed the critics and were soon the toast of the five boroughs. Al made more than enough money to start Writers House from a season of sell-out shows.

Of course he would have given everything back if it could have prolonged Chenille's life by even an hour. Sadly, she passed away in her sleep at age sixteen. When Sir Albert told me this story, he finished by unbuttoning his shirt and showing me the faded tattoo of a small Pekingese puppy positioned perfectly over his heart. He looked me square in the eye and said, "BTG, in this life you will come to know and befriend many people. Some will be brave, and some will be funny. Some will be short; some will be tall. Some will be younger, like you, and some will be older, like me. Some will offer you bread and wine; some will offer you marzipan even though you don't like it. Never judge them. The important thing is that you are true to your friends, always. And never miss an opportunity to thank them for sharing their life with you. And if you are true and if you are kind and grateful, then maybe, just maybe, you will have found a friend to the end."

Al, what did I do to deserve a friend like you?

Friends to the End

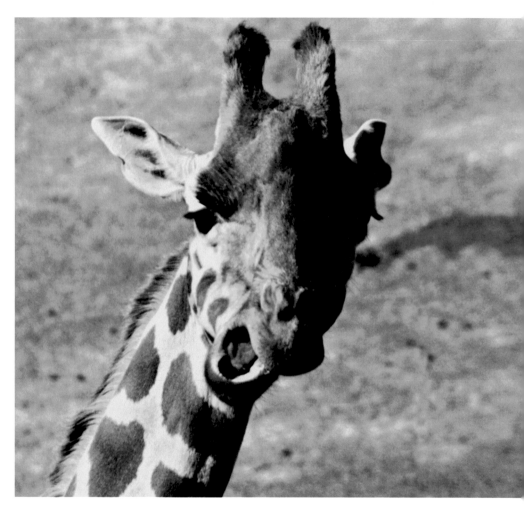

It's not easy finding the words
to talk about a friendship like ours,

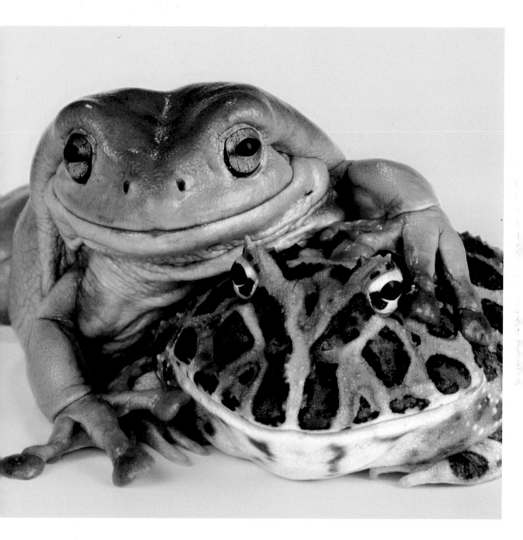

which is strange, considering how close we have become.

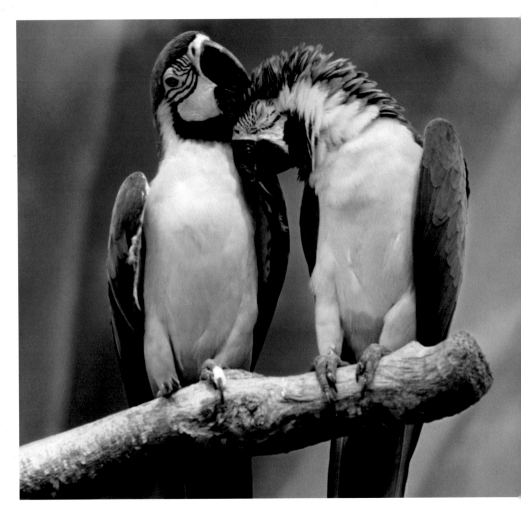

There have been so many times
when we both needed a shoulder to cry on

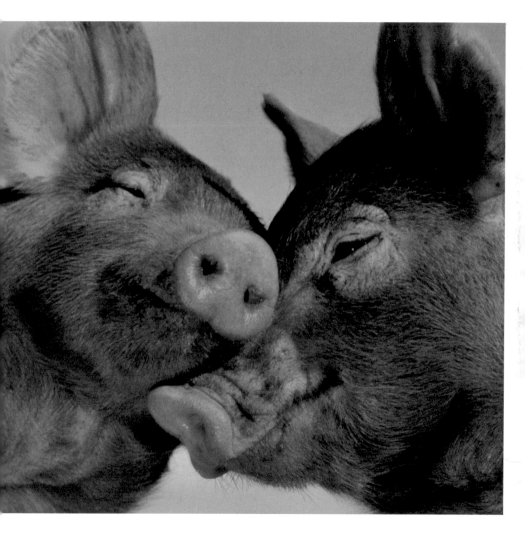

or a snout to sigh on . . . and so forth.

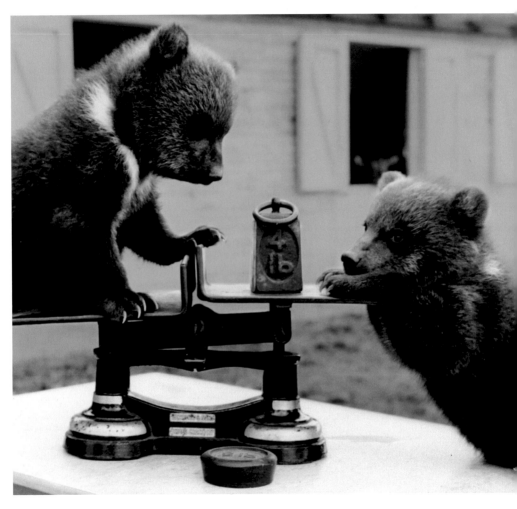

It makes me wonder, how can we possibly express
what friends are really worth?

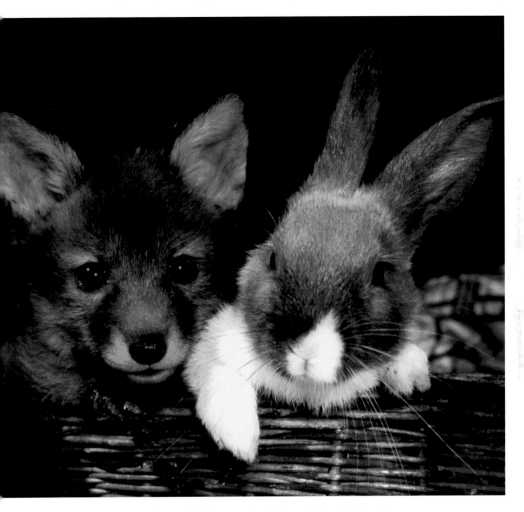

What makes friendship, especially a friendship like ours, so special?

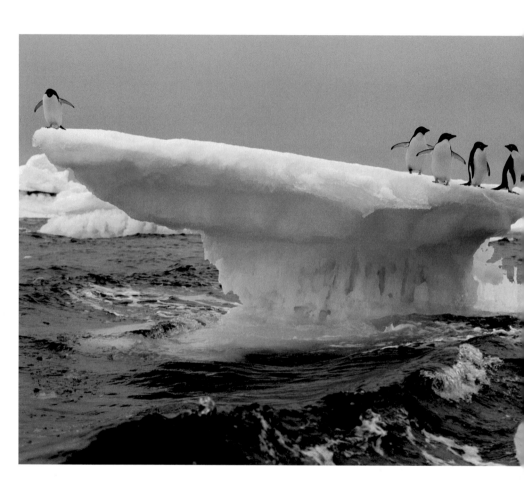

Contrary to popular belief,
it is actually possible to survive without friends.

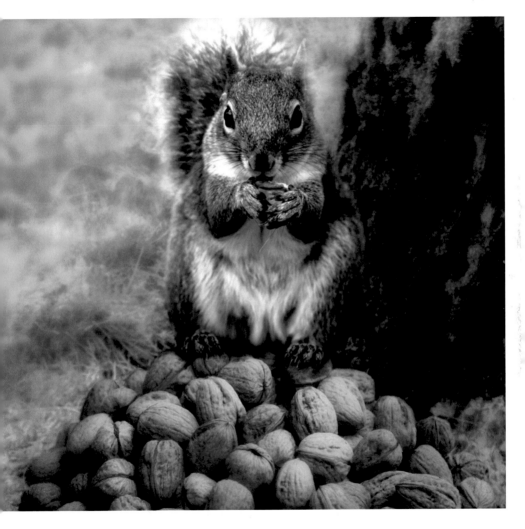

Indeed, there are a few genuine advantages to being alone,

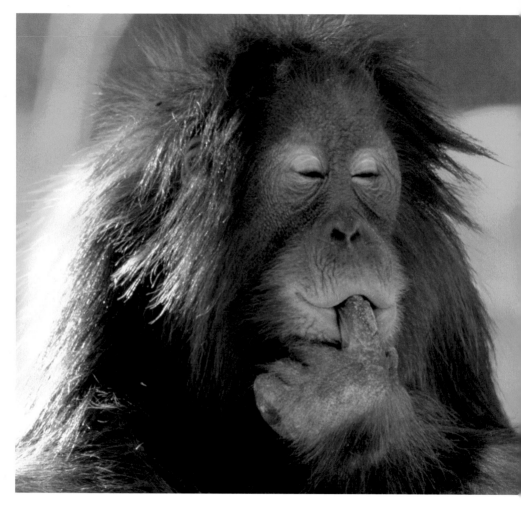

and there are also some activities that, frankly,
shouldn't involve anybody else.

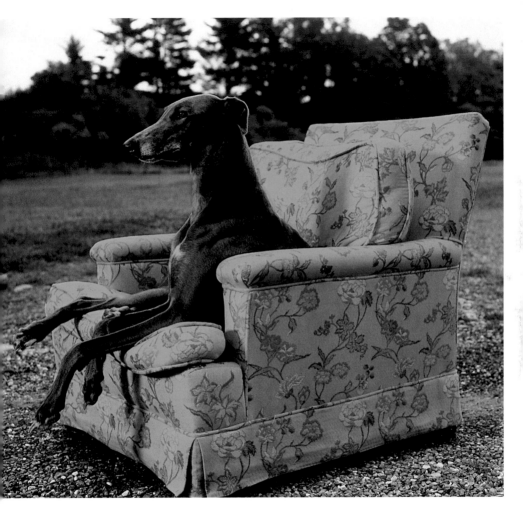

It's a scientific fact that time spent in quiet isolation
thinking about our lives is vital to a healthy state of mind,

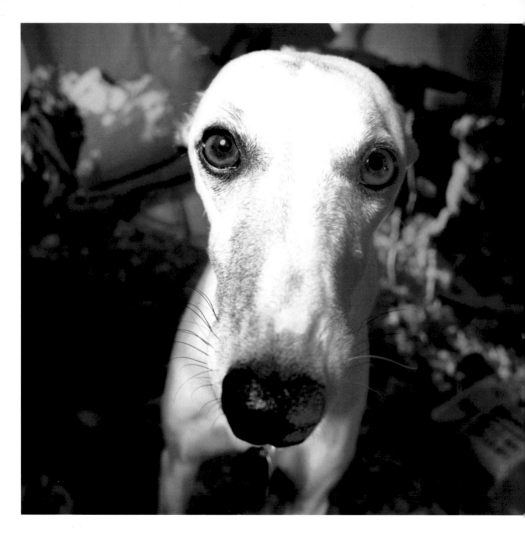

as long as we don't do too much of it.

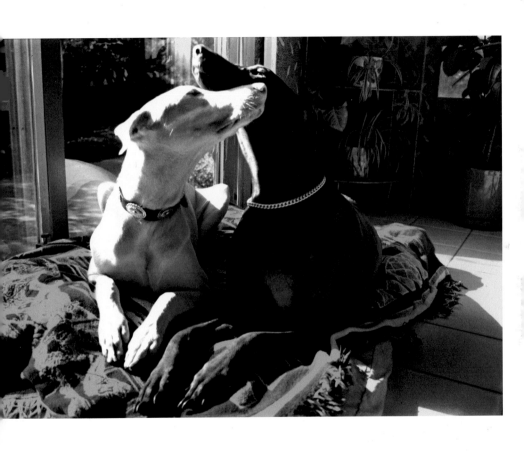

At the end of the day, we are social creatures

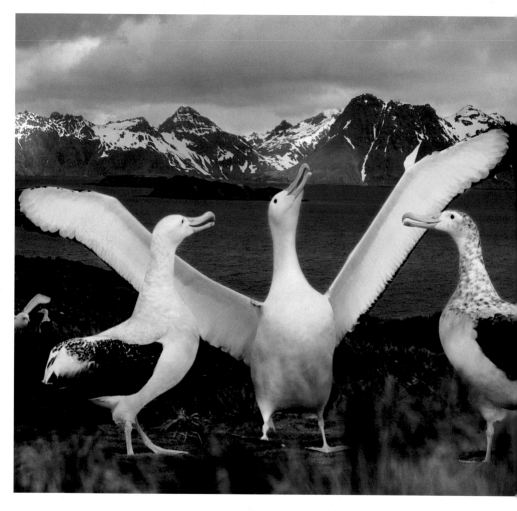

who find that being with other people
and bringing people together are very fulfilling experiences.

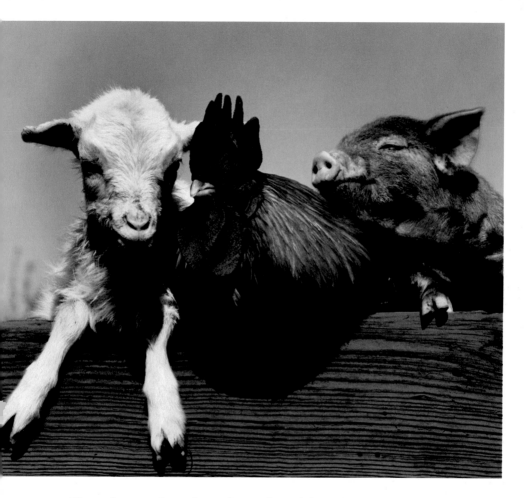

There is a curious fact about friendship that we have
always known but rarely acknowledge: By understanding others,
we also come closer to understanding ourselves.

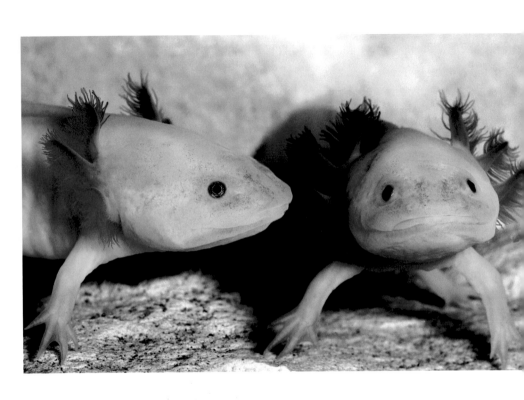

What we look for and value in our friends are the very same qualities
we are most proud of or wish were more evident in ourselves.

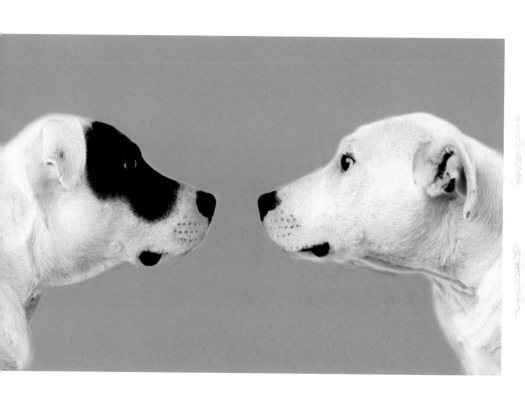

So in no small way, our friends tell us a lot about who we are

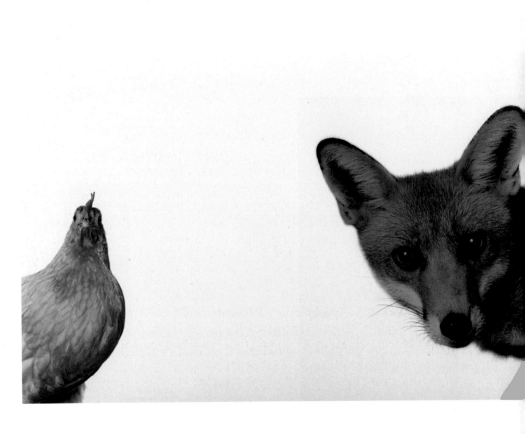

and who we aren't.

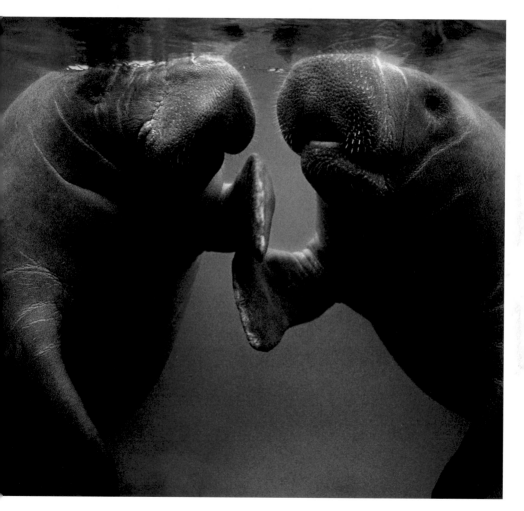

We all have many different types of friends—from the person
we simply smile at and high-five over the water cooler

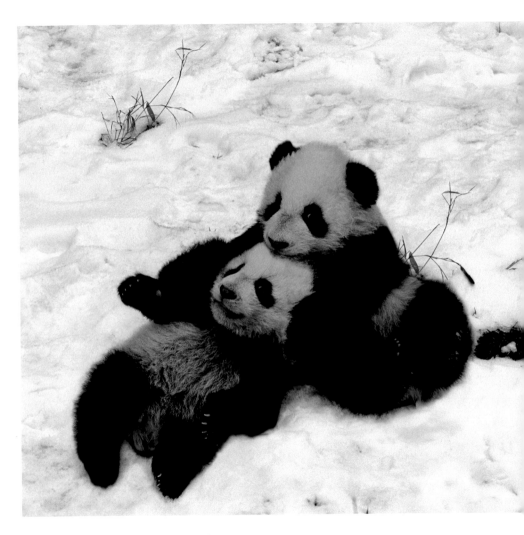

to our childhood pals.

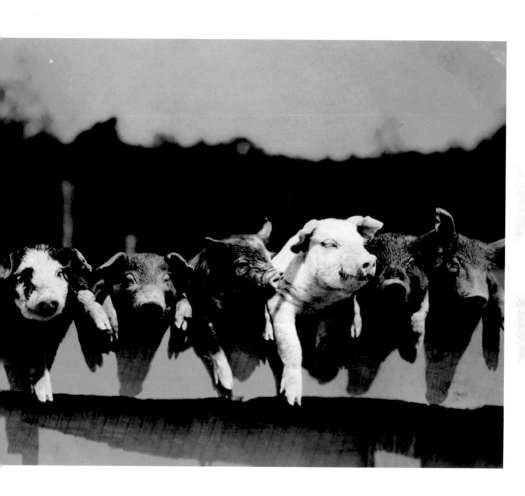

There is "the gang" we hang out with from time to time

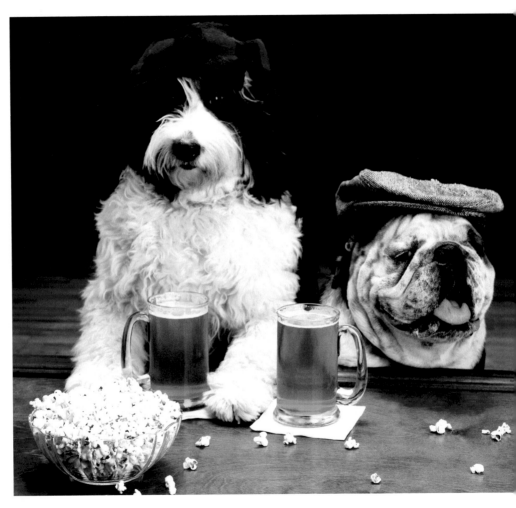

and the buddies with whom we deconstruct the workweek over a relaxing aperitif or an episode of *Sex and the City* or both.

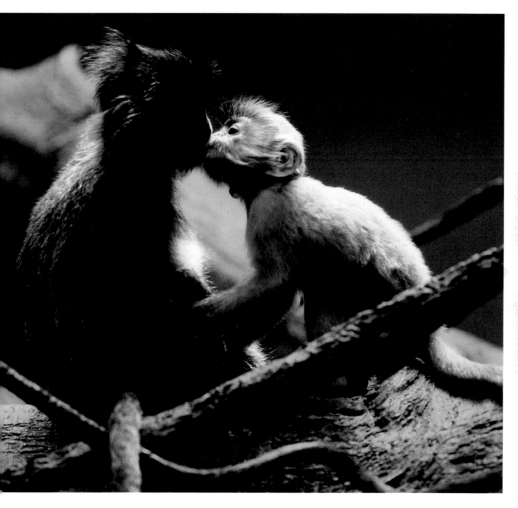

There are also the lucky individuals with whom
we are especially close,

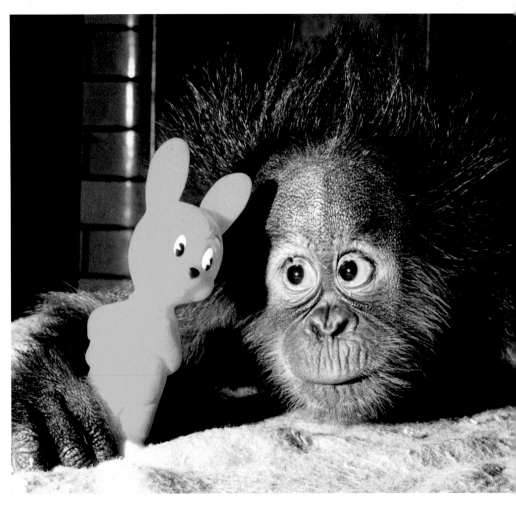

and there are even imaginary friends. (But now we are starting
to enter *Jerry Springer* territory . . . so we'll just move right along.)

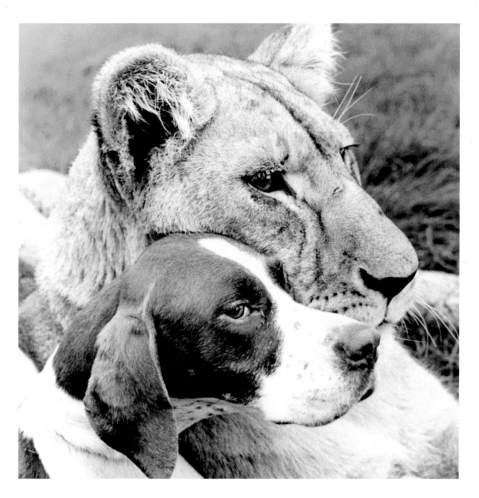

Genuine friendships are founded on a shared vision—
the view that our lives are somehow better
because particular people are part of them.

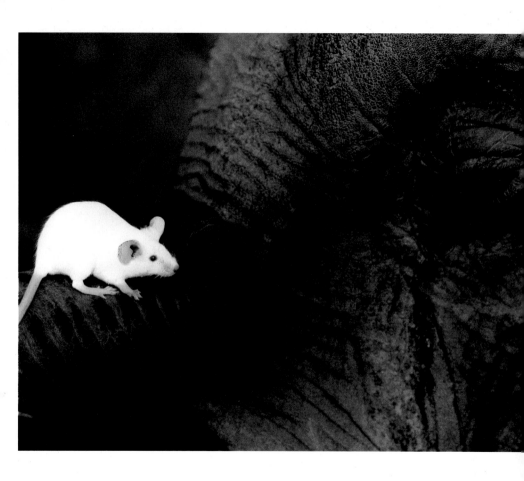

Despite numerous differences, real friends see eye to eye
on all the issues that matter. Our common values, passions, concerns,
and mutual respect enhance our life experiences as a whole.

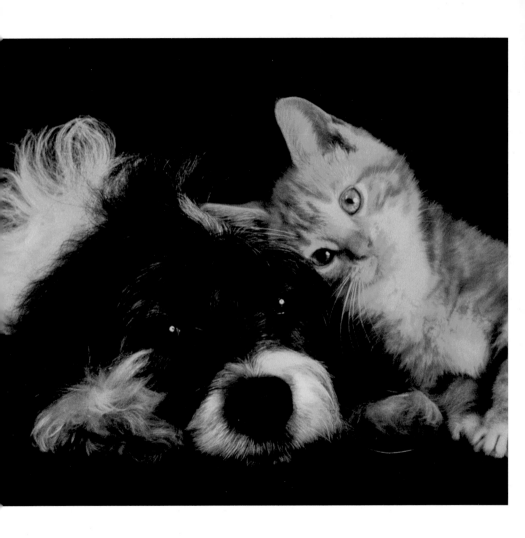

Friends genuinely care about each other.

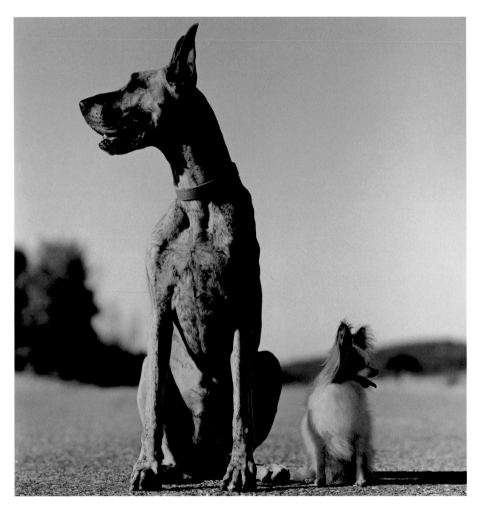

We can always count on our pals to watch our back
and look out for our best interests.

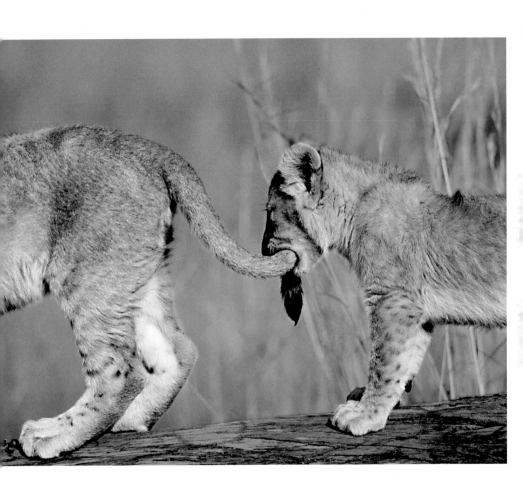

This faith in our friends grows as each of us
helps the other move forward in life.

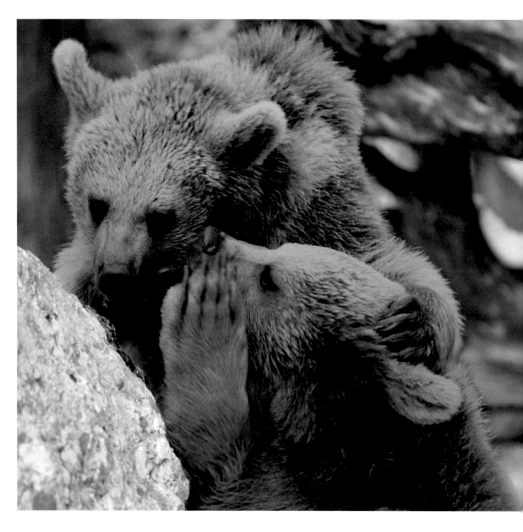

It's the same trust we count on when we share secrets,

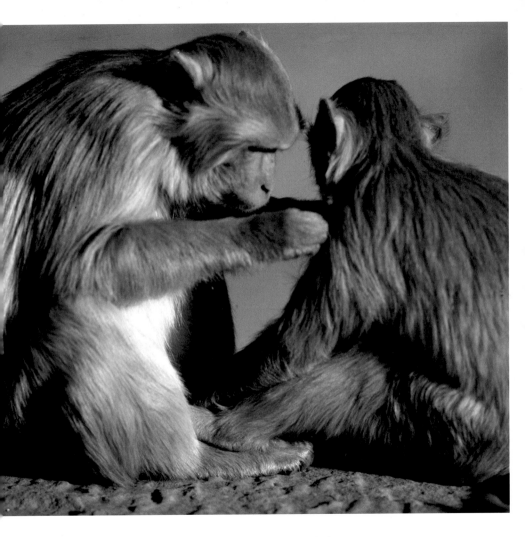

ask if our tie is on straight,

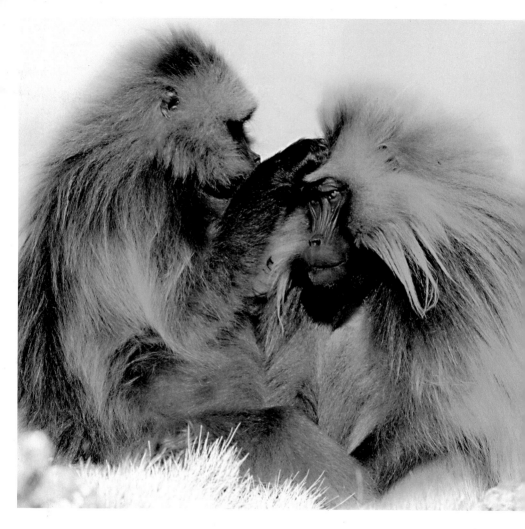

or need our hair teased *just* so.

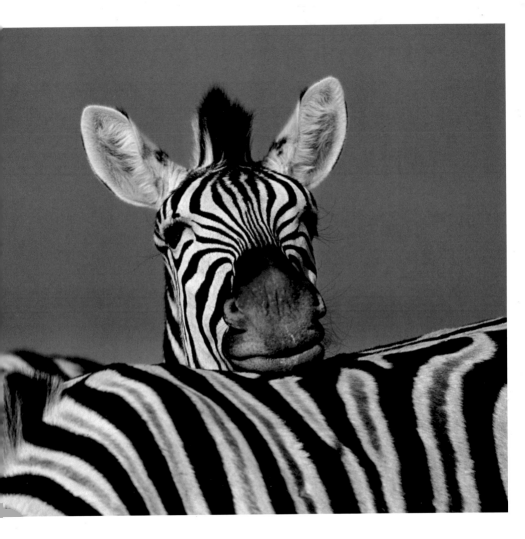

A friend is there to help keep our chin up, no matter what it takes.

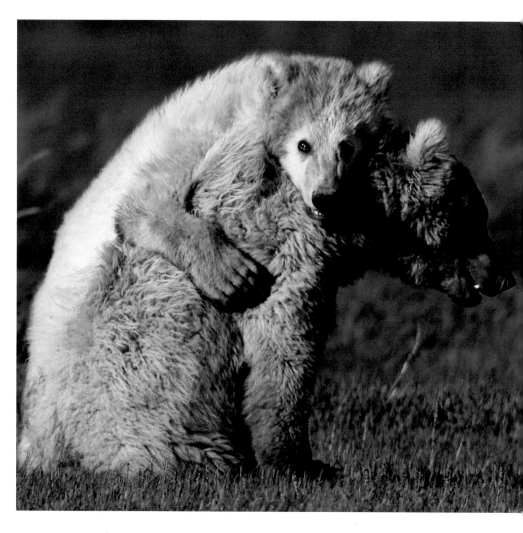

A friend knows when we need a hug

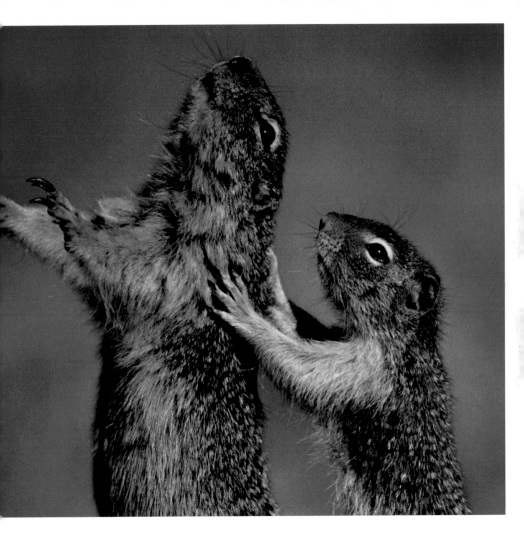

or a tension-relieving back rub.

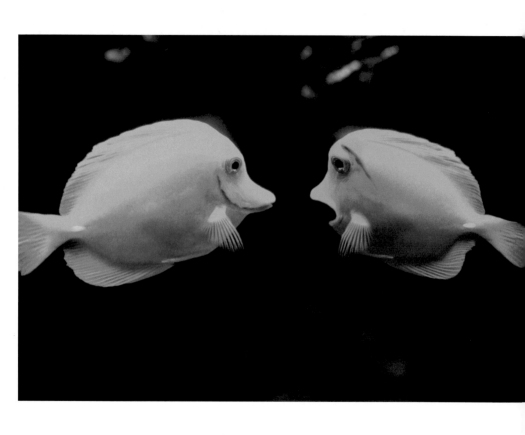

Friends know when to offer serious counsel
and thoughtful, heartfelt advice,

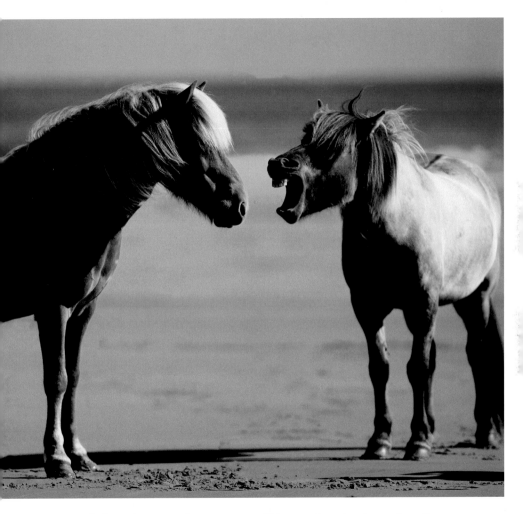

and they know when to say, "Hey, why the long face?
Snap out of it!"

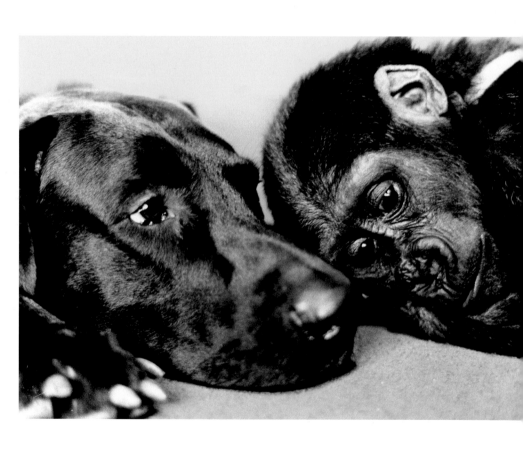

Most important, friends know when to just sit quietly beside us
and say nothing at all.

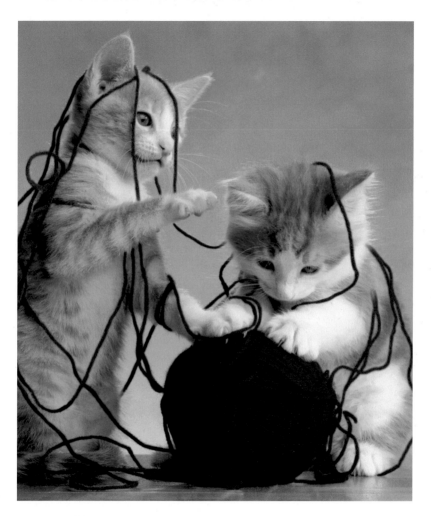

Obviously, the best thing about our friends
is that we have fun together. Lots of fun.

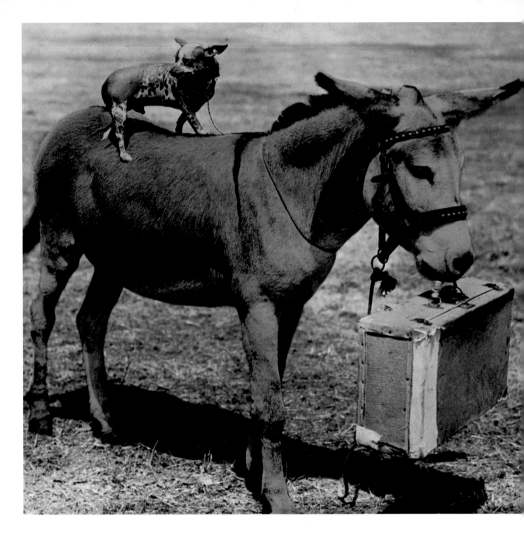

We go on adventures,

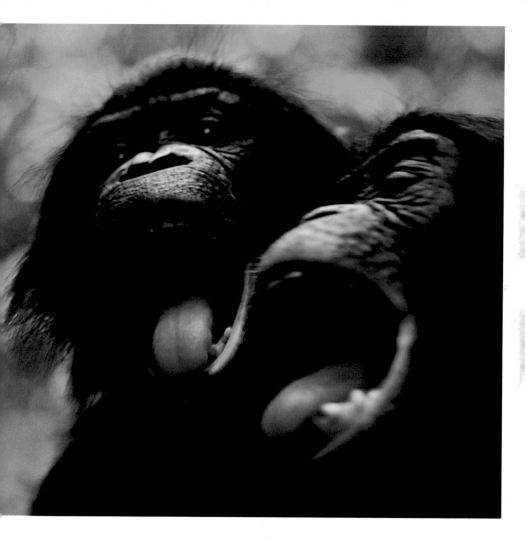

scream out the lyrics at Bon Jovi concerts,

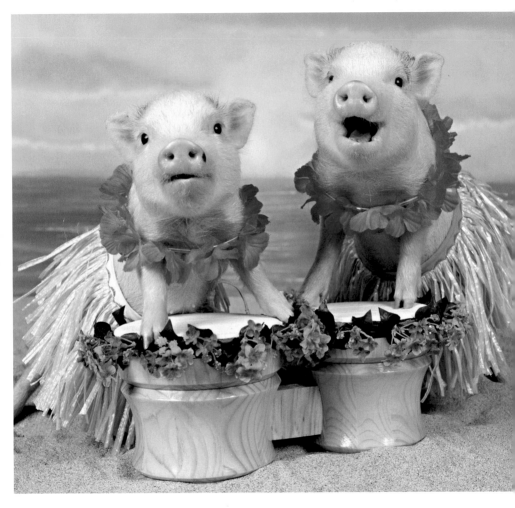

and basically get ourselves into bizarre but enjoyable situations
that probably don't make a lot of sense to anybody else.

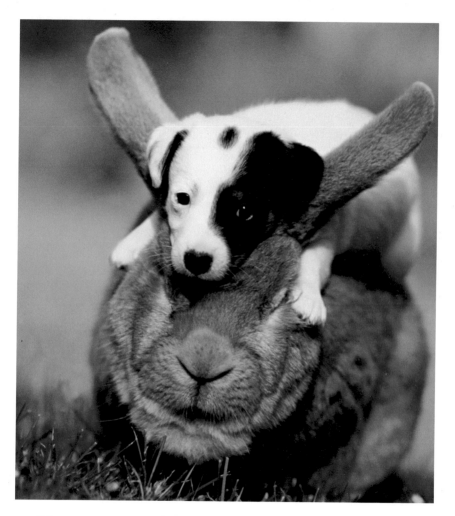

Of course, every relationship of note comes with a price.
Some friends need so much support they become a burden.

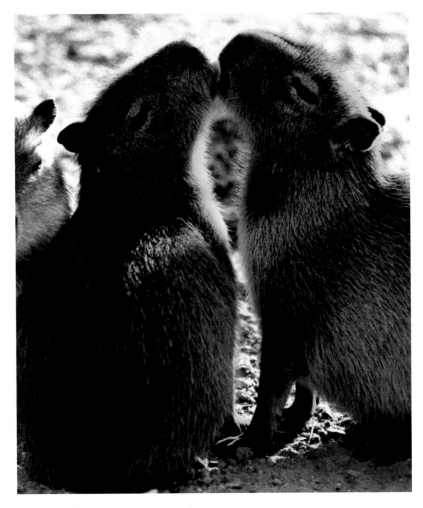

Even soul mates can't agree on absolutely everything all the time.
This is just something we have to accept.

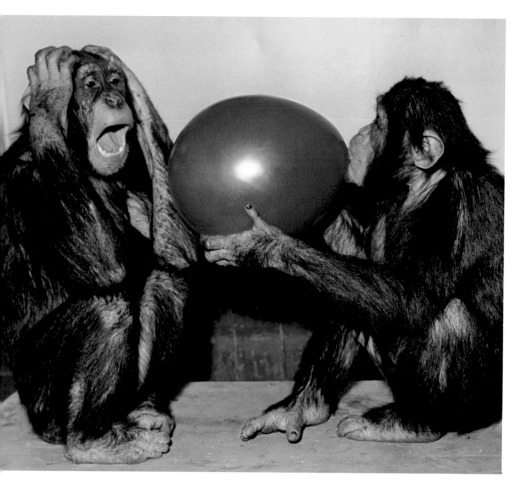

In fact, there are occasions when our friends,
knowing us as well as they do, seem as if they are deliberately
trying to drive us crazy.

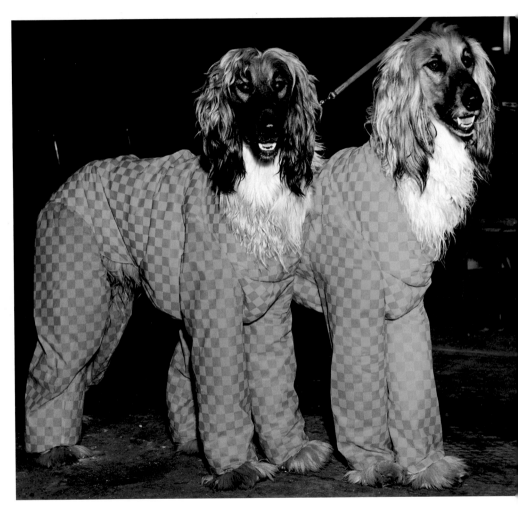

Some friends develop an unhealthy admiration
for our personal fashion sense

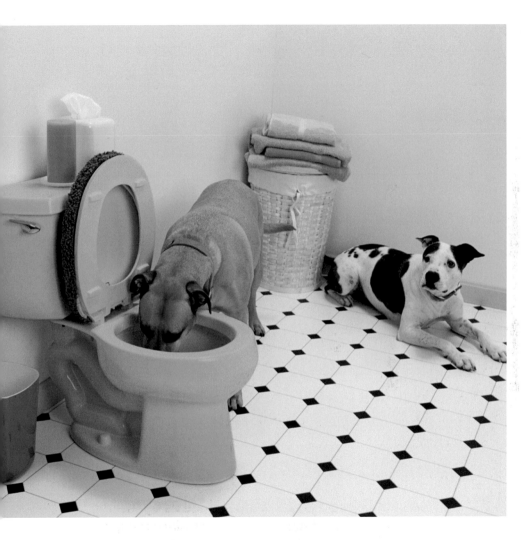

or just have gross habits they simply cannot kick.

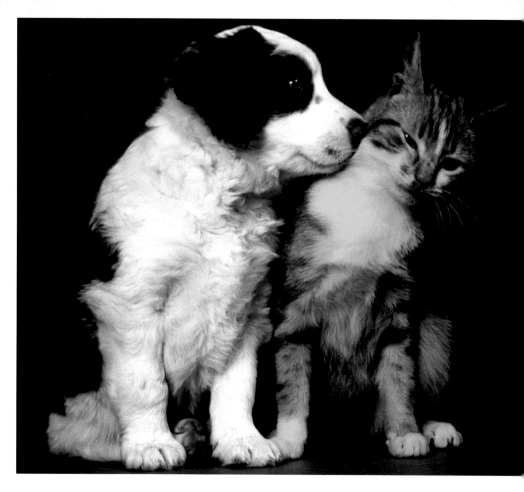

Even our closest friends can unhinge us by insisting on
setting us up with blind dates who are as alarmingly inappropriate
as they are enthusiastic

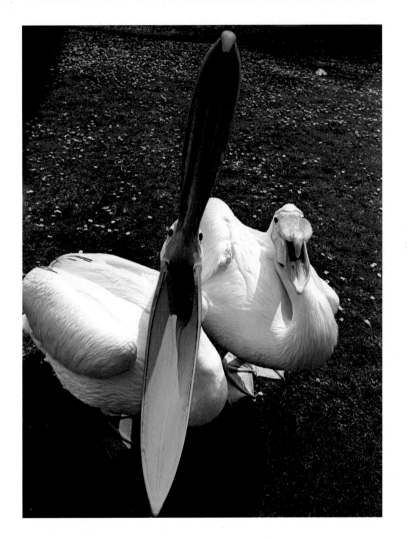

or by opening their big mouths at inopportune moments,

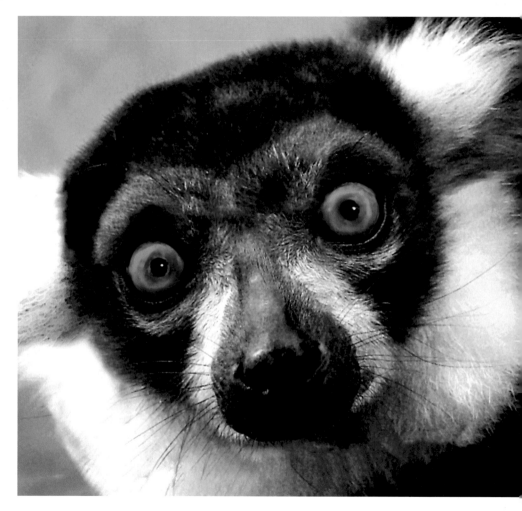

and suddenly everyone at the office knows you always wear
"lucky" leopard-print underwear on a third date.

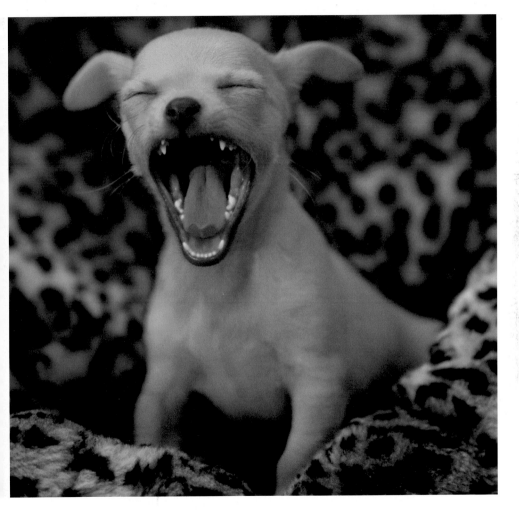

Nevertheless, after a suitable period of time in self-imposed exile
where we can scream until our tonsils shatter,

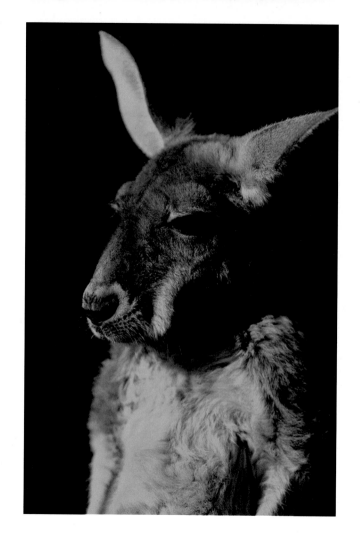

we eventually shrug our shoulders, forgive them, and move on.

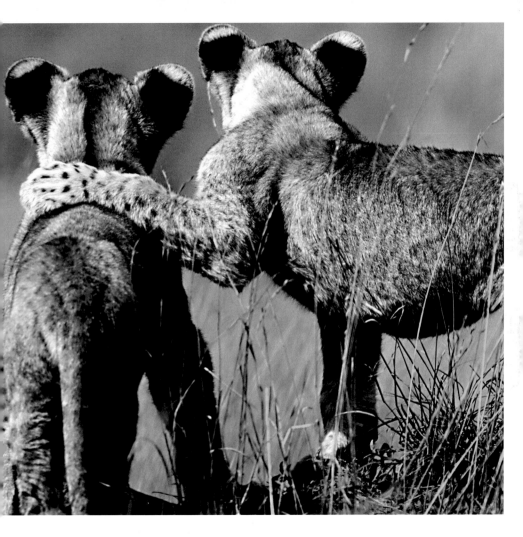

Because that's just what friends do.

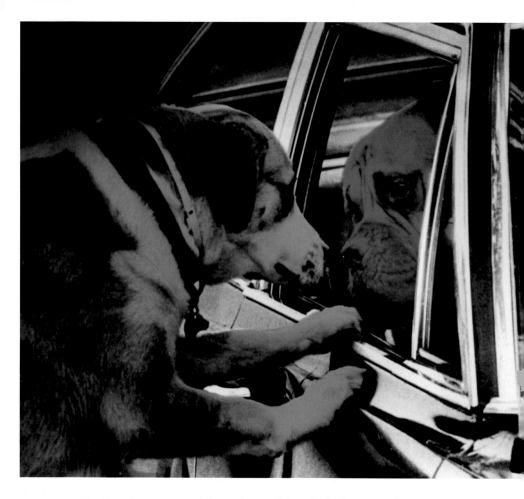

By far the worst thing about friends is having them leave.
Whether they move to another city or to another country,
this is the saddest of good-byes,

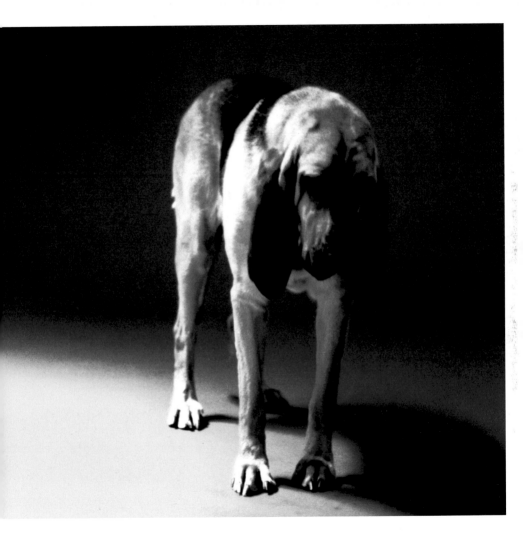

especially if we know we have seen them for the very last time.

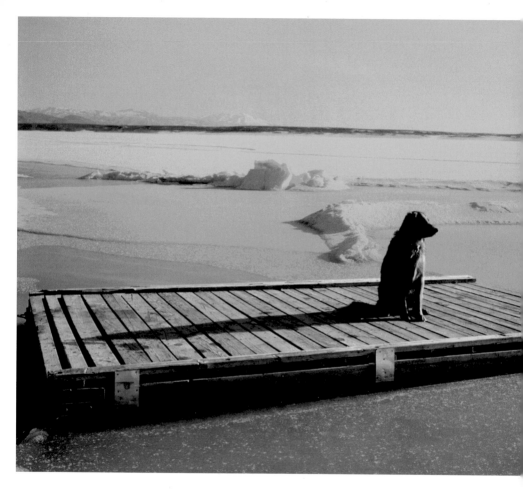

Thinking about losing friends, though it makes us feel incredibly sad, is actually very healthy if it reminds us how special our friends are and that they cannot be replaced.

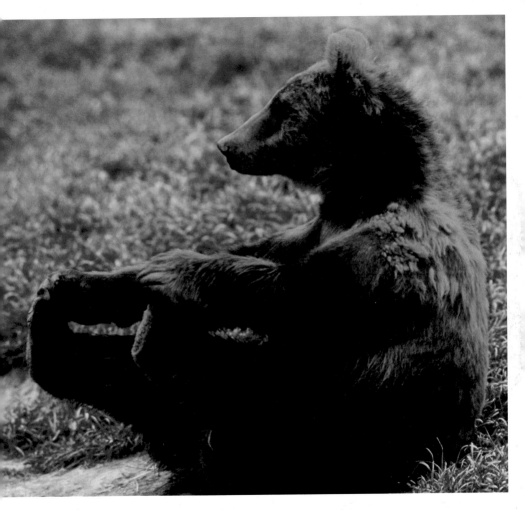

You could search the whole world looking for a friendship like ours,
and you would only wear out a good pair of feet.

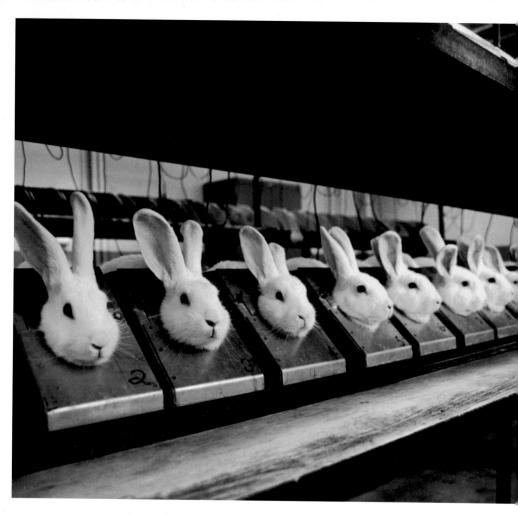

Great friends cannot be manufactured in a laboratory by an evil genius.

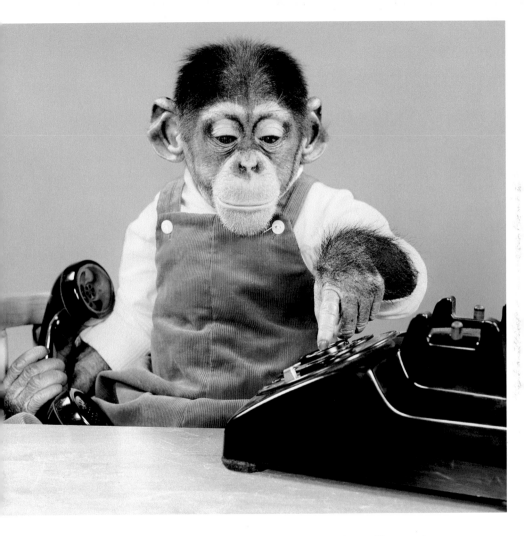

We cannot order a friend delivered to our door like a pizza

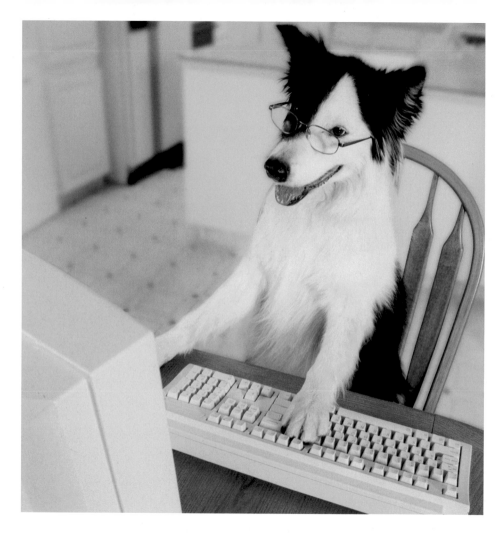

or download one from the Internet.

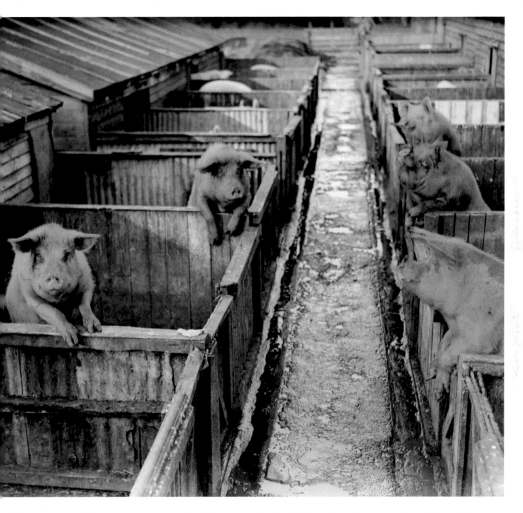

However, there are potentially wonderful friends all over the place just waiting to be met. We could find them at the office;

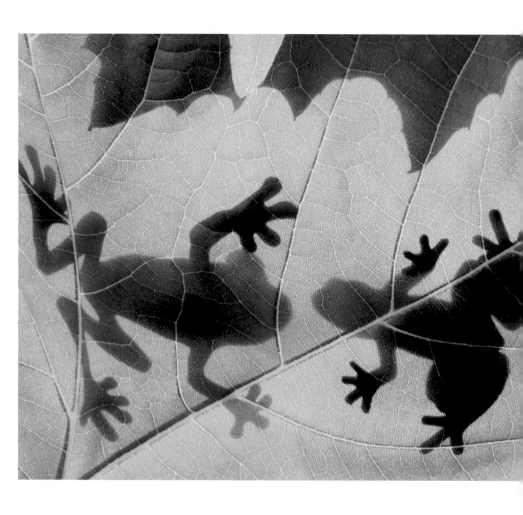

we could stumble across them in the park;

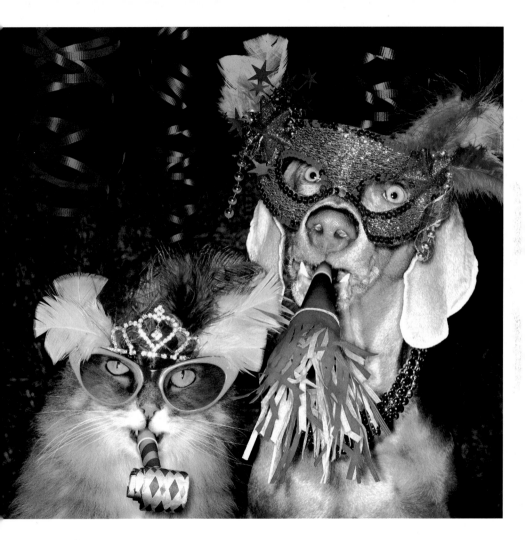

we could meet them at a quiet soiree. Who knows?

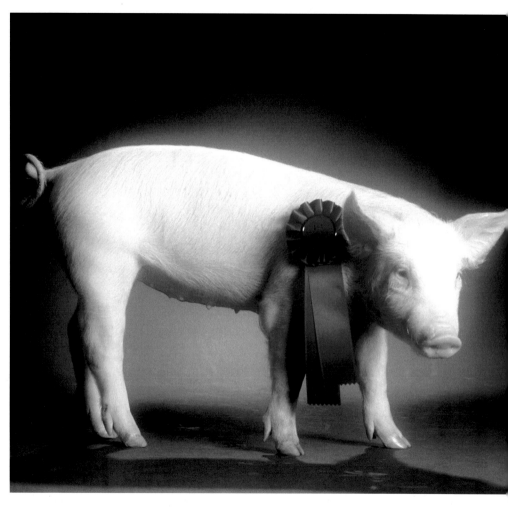

It is usually not possible to tell at first sight whether we will get along with

someone or not. There are no "ready-made perfect friends" per se.

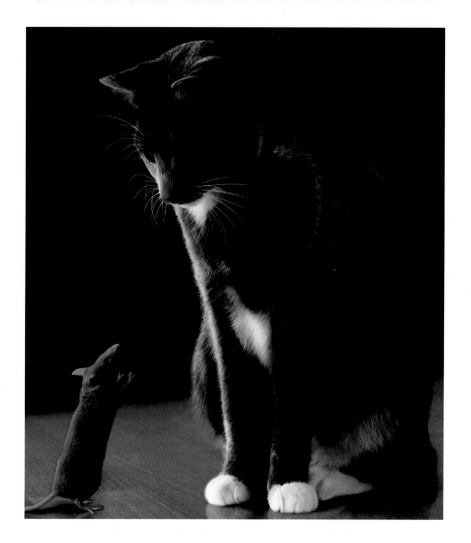

There are simply people to whom we can really pour out our hearts

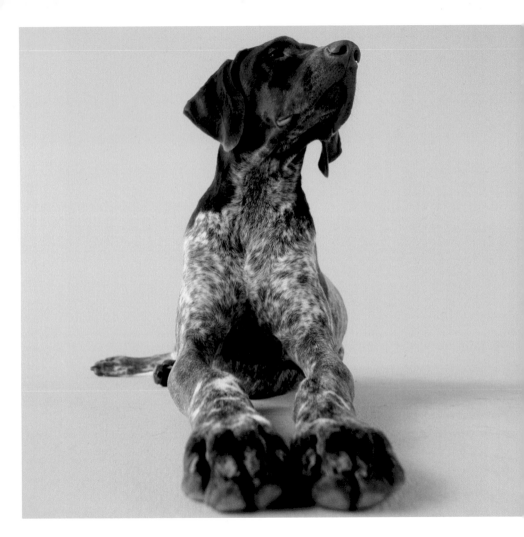

and those we can't.

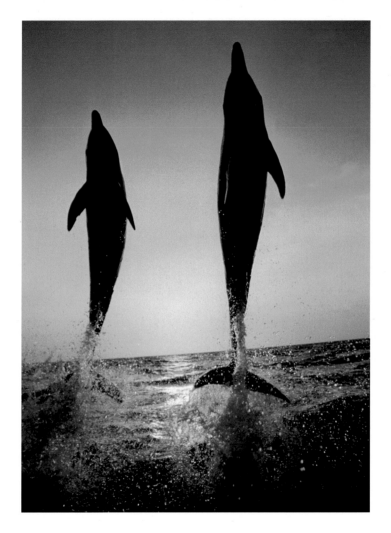

There are individuals who invigorate and inspire us

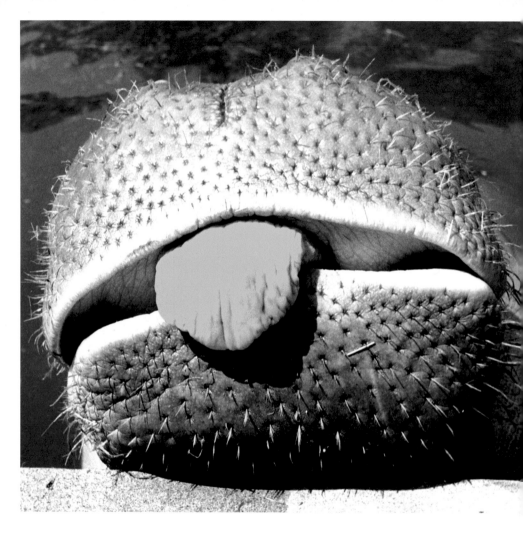

and those who bore us to death.

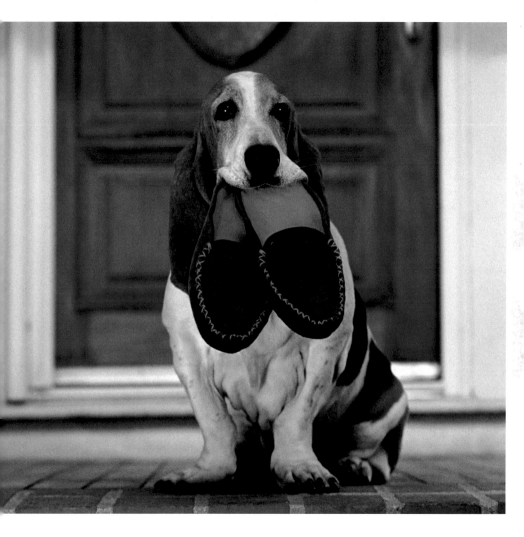

There are folks who really make us feel comfortable

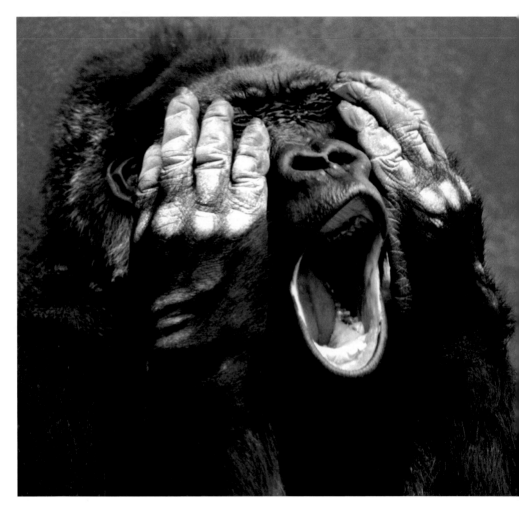

and others who frustrate, aggravate, and infuriate us
to the point of madness.

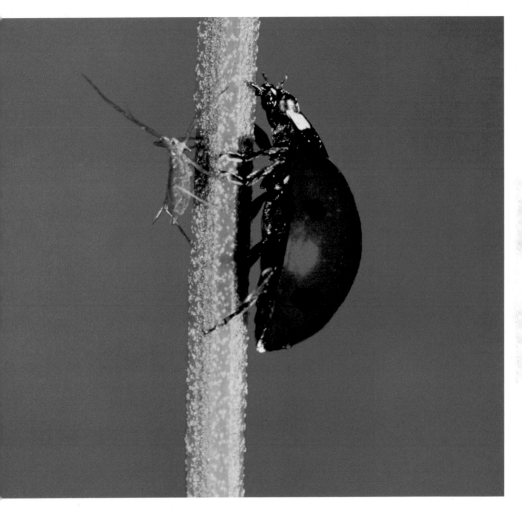

A real friendship is something we both have to build—
in many ways it's a journey we take together.

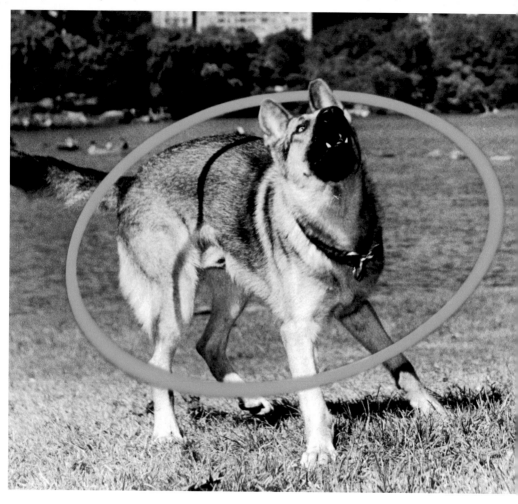

The key to starting on the right foot
is not to try and impress anybody.

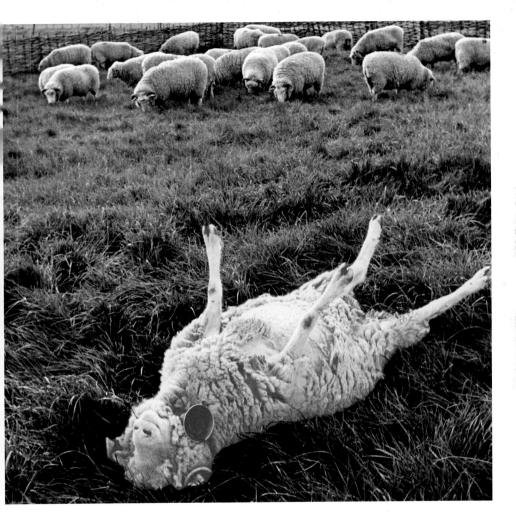

No one can keep up the act forever, so you may as well
just be yourself from day one—they can like it or lump it.

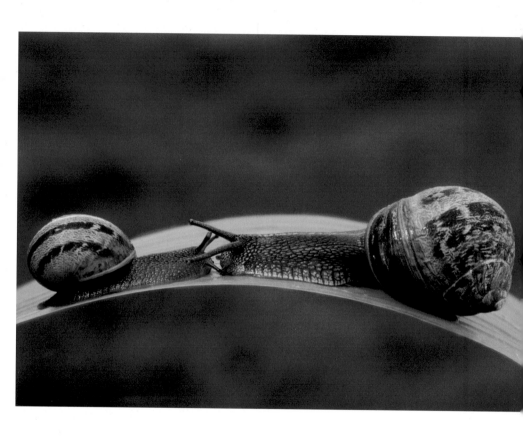

Take your time getting to know each other. What's the hurry?

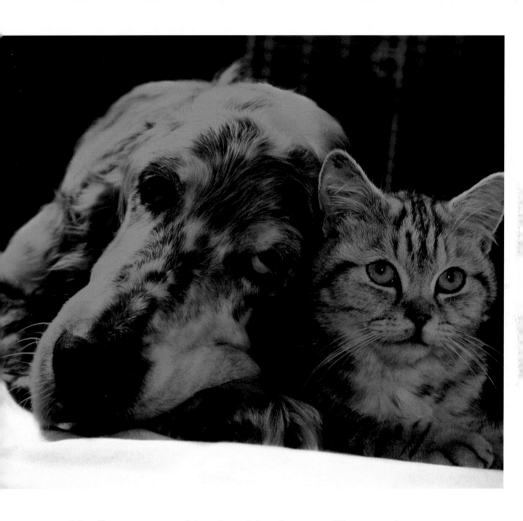

Ideally, we want friends with whom we'll grow closer
and closer as we get older,

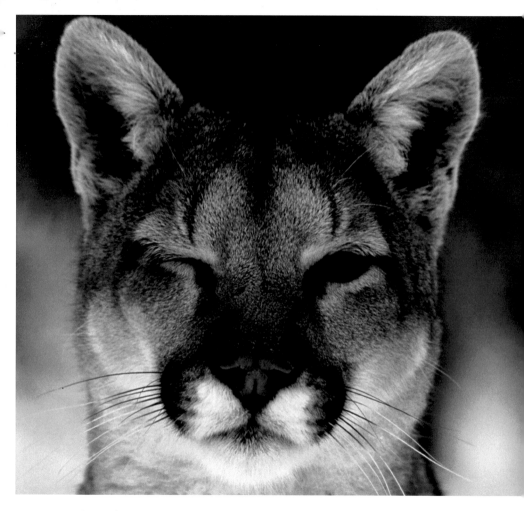

so it makes sense to invest a little time and energy finding out who they really are.

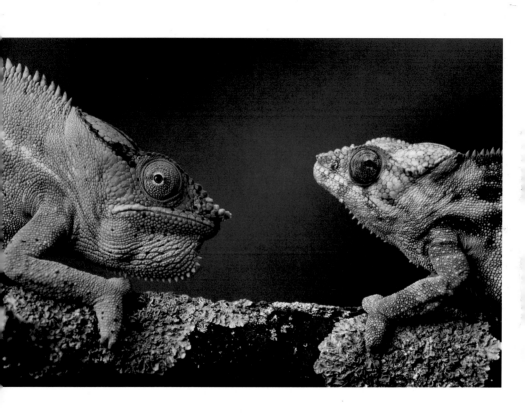

After a few conversations, you may find that
despite all the indications, you really have nothing in common.

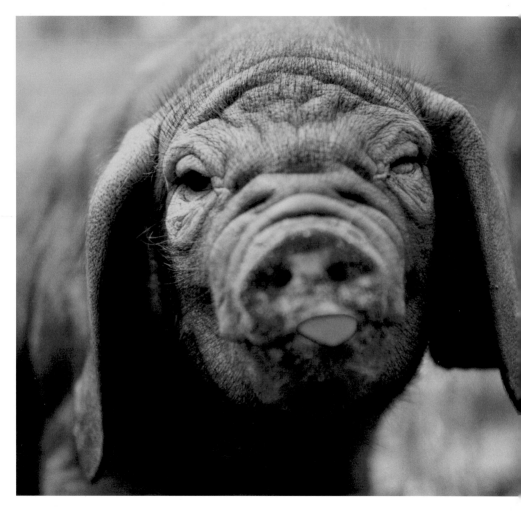

You may also unearth an ugly side of their personalities
that you weren't aware of.

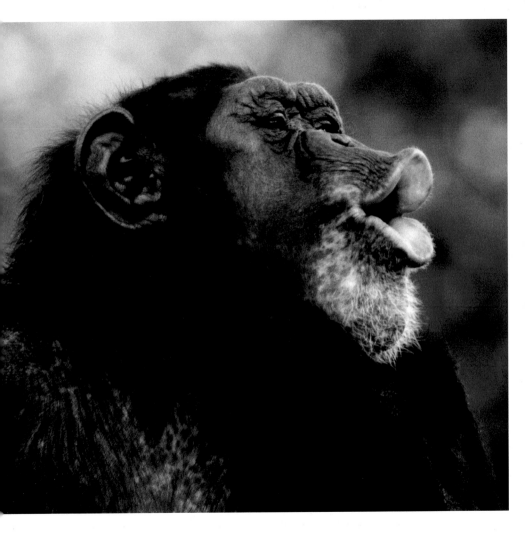

They may turn out to be chronic air-kissers,

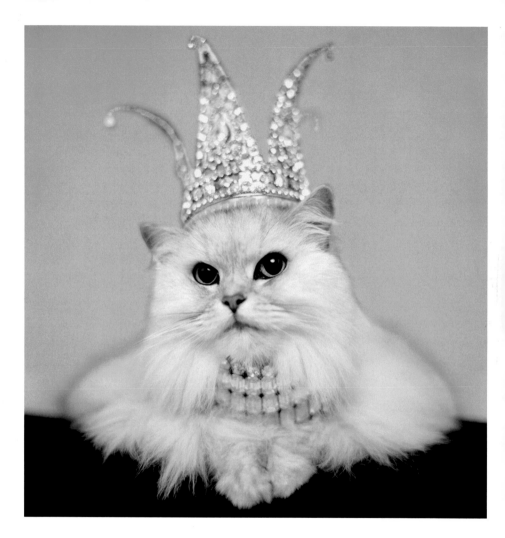

unbearable drama queens,

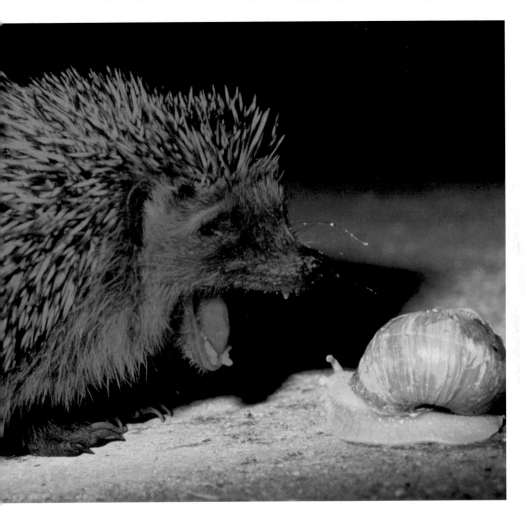

or bullies who bite your head off
whenever things don't go their way.

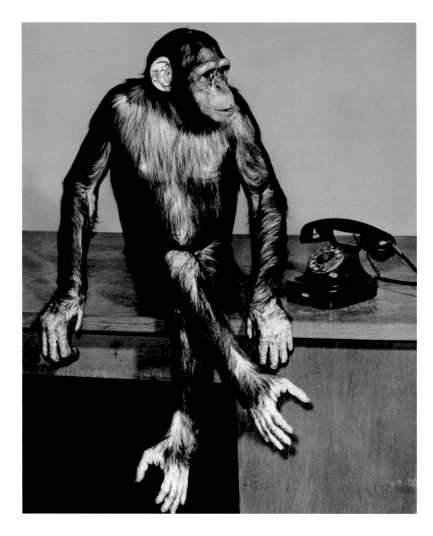

They may become unreliable, forgetting to call

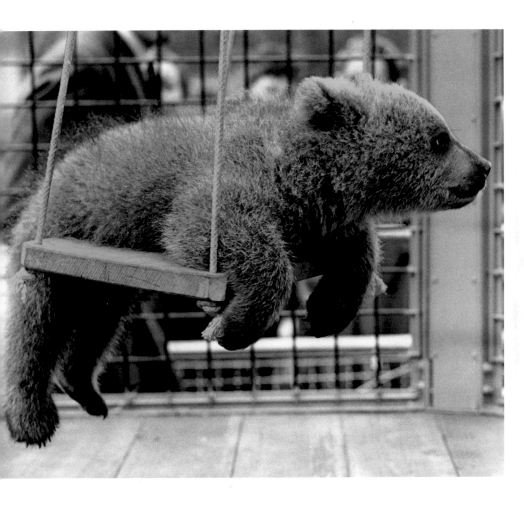

and then leaving you hanging
after you have canceled all your other plans,

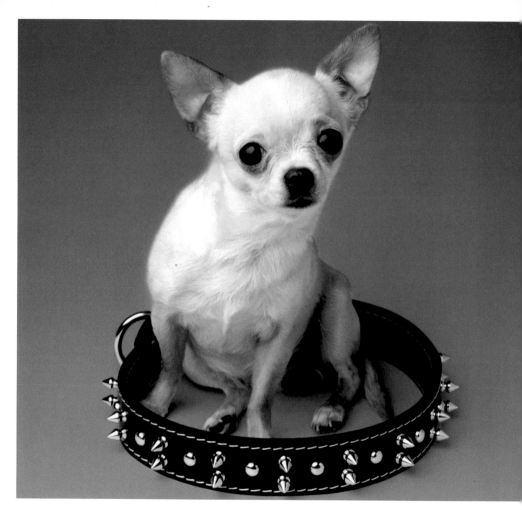

which causes your self-esteem to plummet
to unfathomable new depths.

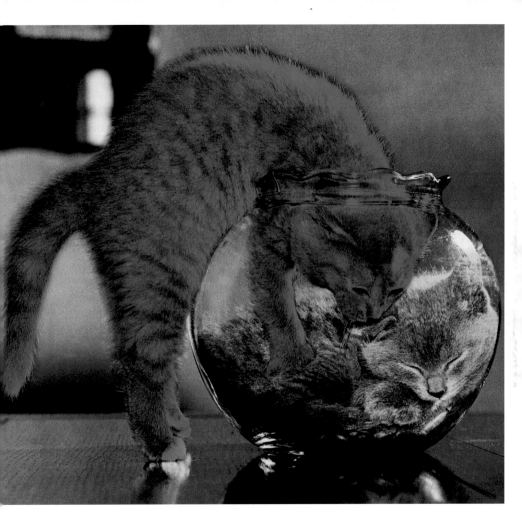

Then again, they may like you too much,
smothering you with excessive affection

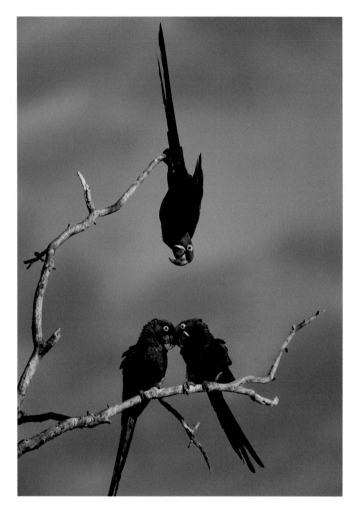

and finding it impossible to accept
that you have other important people in your life.

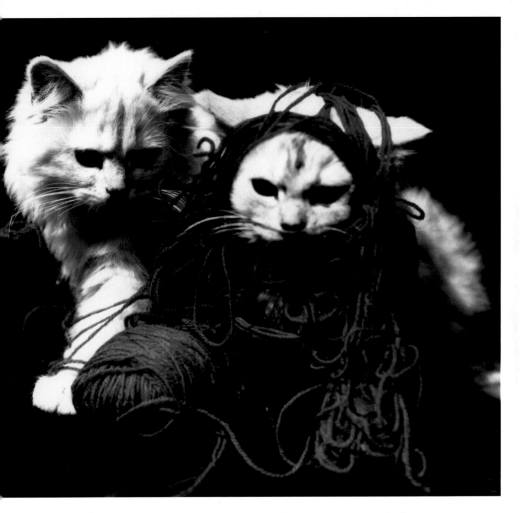

Suddenly, things don't seem to be quite as much fun
as they once were.

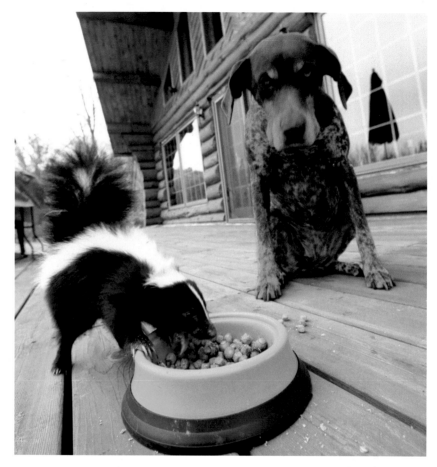

Not all friendships turn out to be really rewarding, but if you end up in a stinker, it's because you've compromised what is really important to you. You cannot be there for anyone else if you are not first true to yourself.

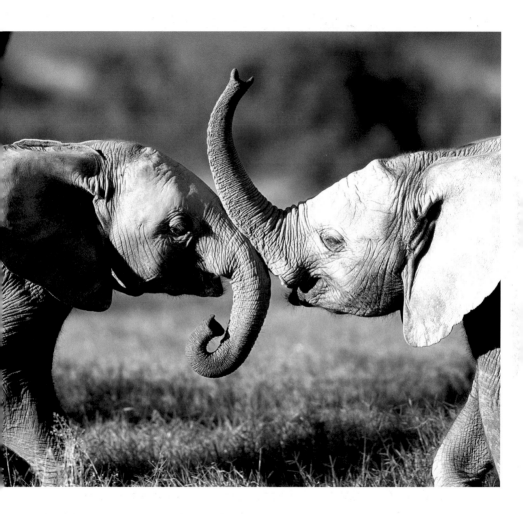

We all want and deserve a friend with whom we truly connect
in a meaningful way.

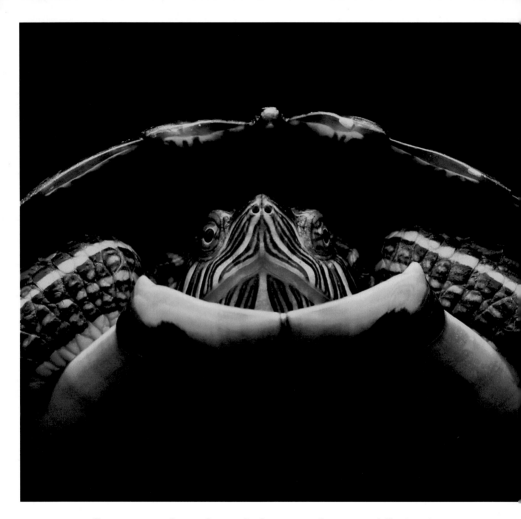

Someone who acknowledges our fears and limitations
without judgment

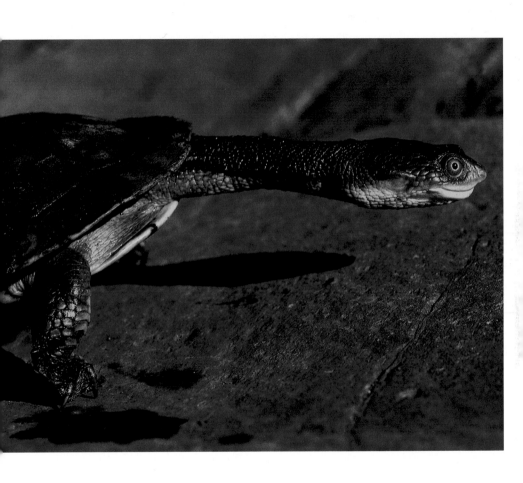

and encourages us to reach further than we ever thought possible.

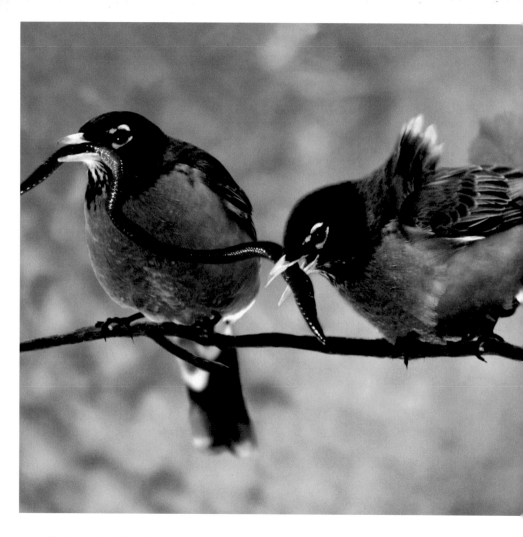

A friend with whom we share things that are most precious to us—

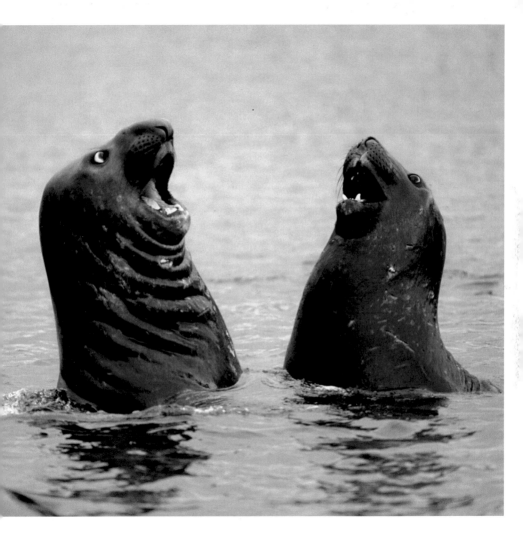

the belly laughs

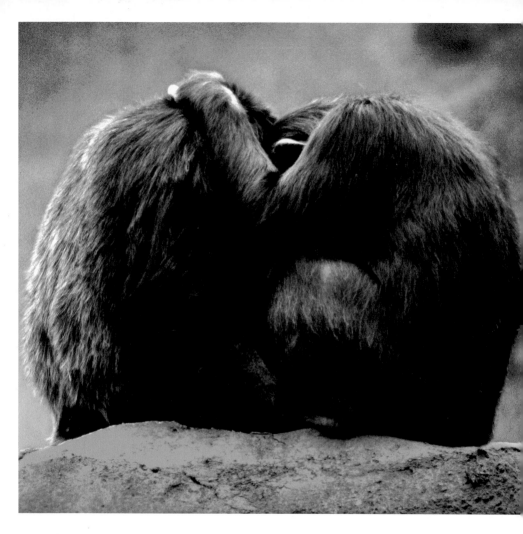

and the sorrows.

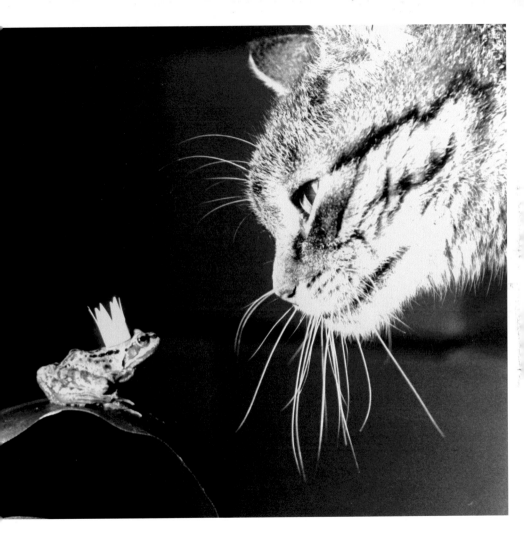

A friend who will see our hidden qualities

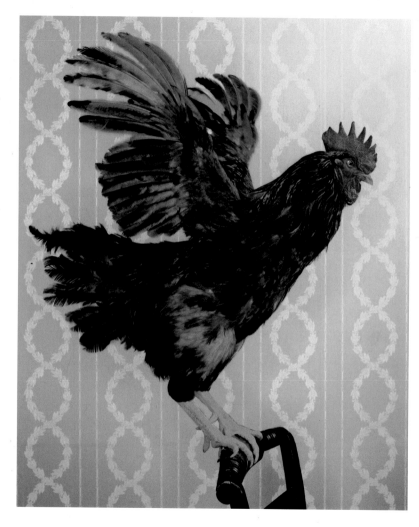

and like us for exactly who we are without reservation,

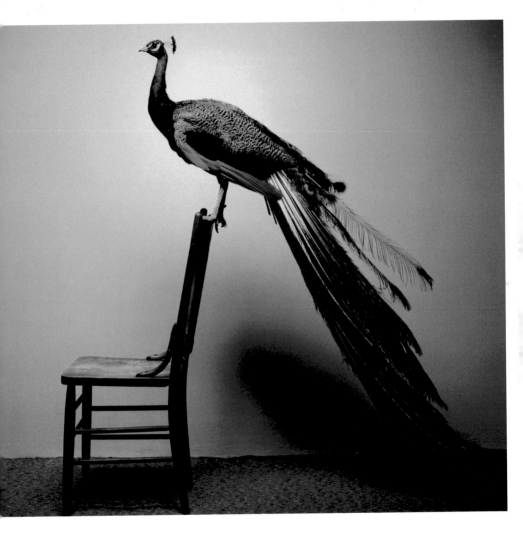

thus helping us fulfill our extraordinary potential.

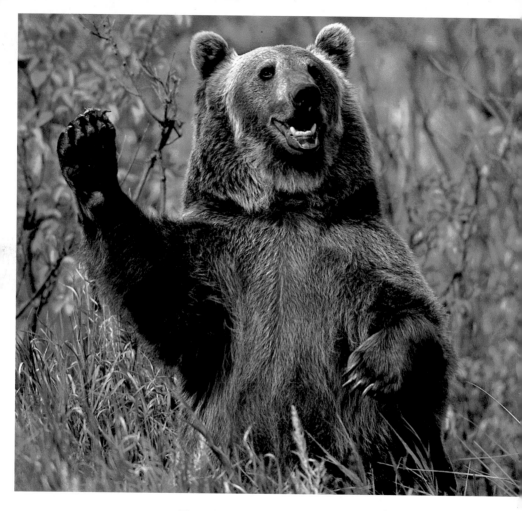

True friends make us smile
as soon as we see them waving to us across a room.

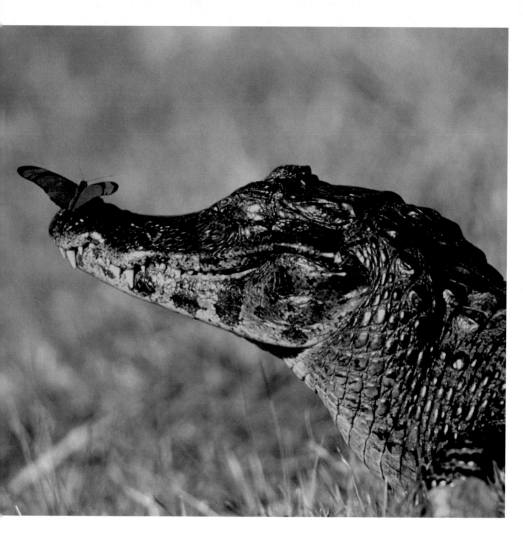

They lighten our hearts without even trying,

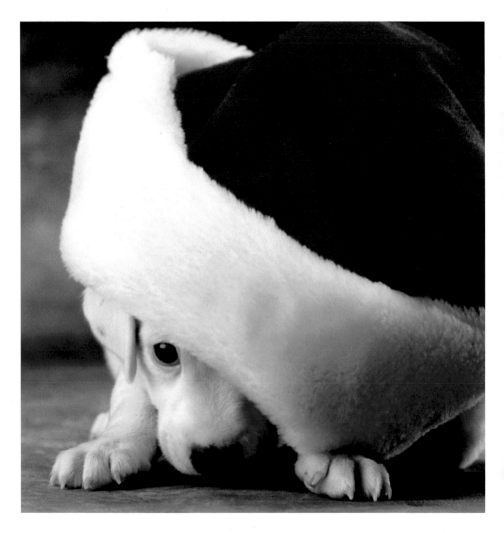

so that time spent together feels like a little slice of Christmas.

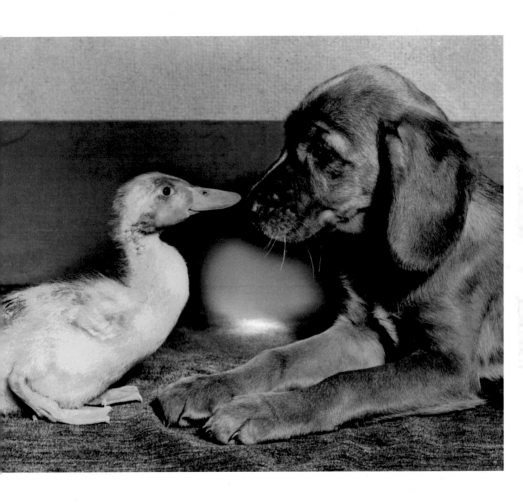

With a real friend, we know exactly what they are thinking
without having to say a word.

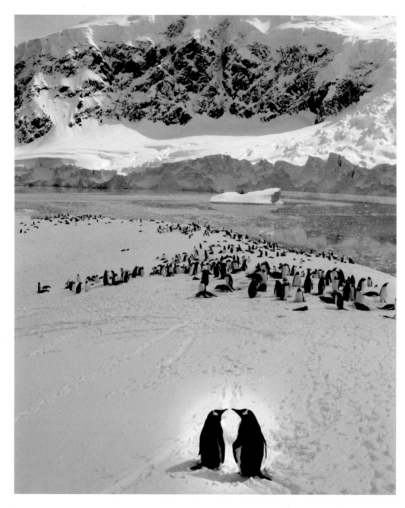

This connection is completely unique. At times it's as if we are the only two people on this earth.

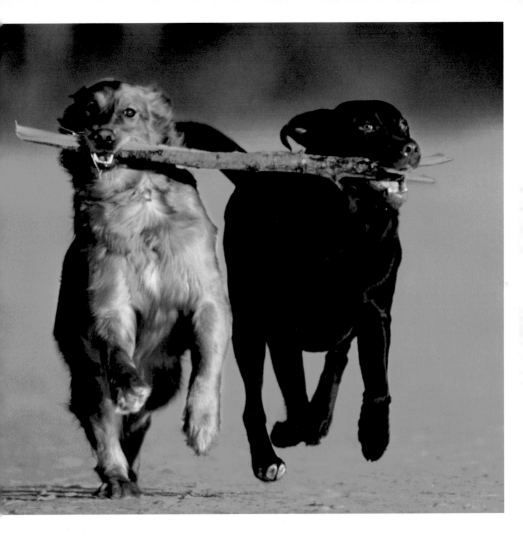

Friendship is a special type of partnership

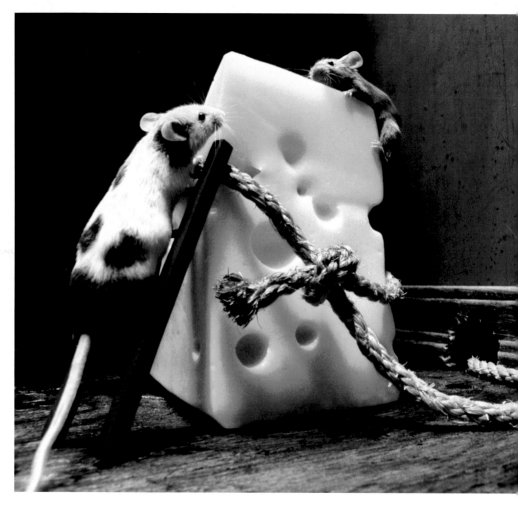

based on the profound understanding that together
the impossible becomes deliciously possible.

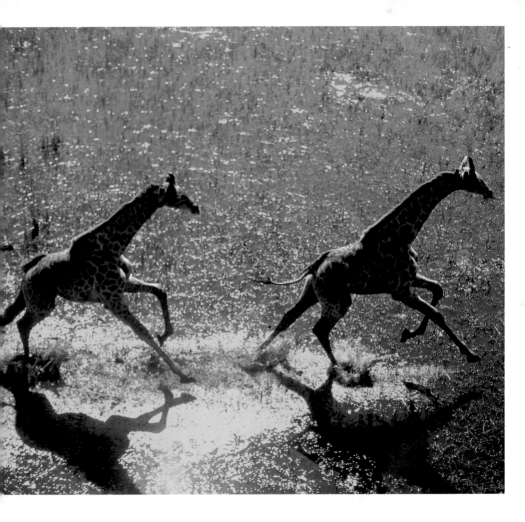

It is an unspoken yet binding commitment to help each other
live our lives to the fullest.

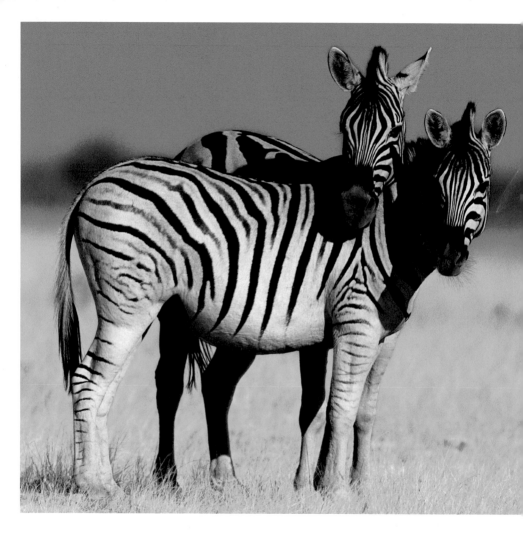

I know how lucky I am to have a friend like that,

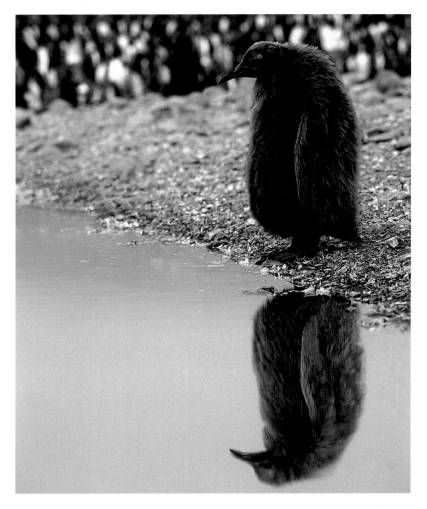

and I just want to say that no matter what happens,
you will never be alone

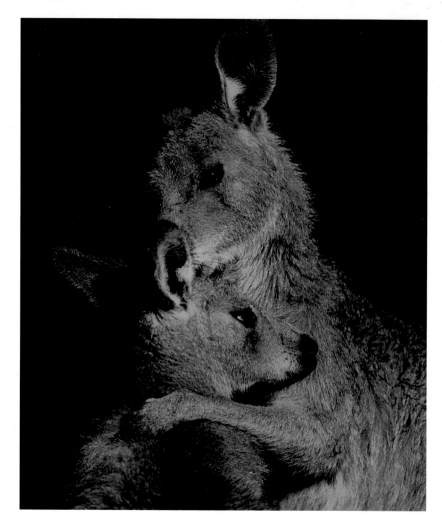

because you will always be my friend.

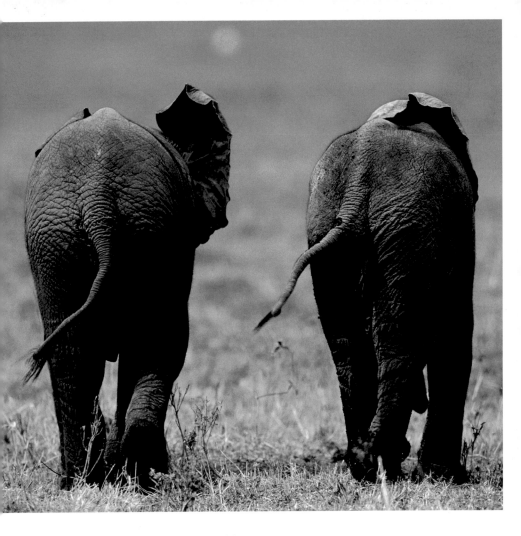

Always.

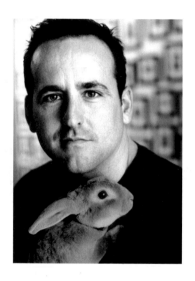

In memory of Biff,
a furry friend to the end